C is for CHRISTMAS

ARRANGED BY ELIZABETH W. GREENLEAF

CONTENTS

Bring a Torch, Jeannette, Isabella

Traditional French Carol

Moderately fast

Teacher Duet: (Student plays 1 octave higher)

He Is Born, The Holy Child

Moderately fast (in 2)

Traditional French Carol

Teacher Duet: (Student plays 1 octave higher)

FF1072

I Saw Three Ships

Moderately fast

Traditional English Carol

Teacher Duet: (Student plays 2 octaves higher)

L.H. warm-up

Jolly Old Saint Nicholas

Quickly

Traditional

Jol - ly old Saint Nich - o - las, lean your ear this way!

Don't you tell a sin - gle soul what I'm going to say;

cross over to A

Christ - mas eve is com - ing soon; now, you dear old man,

Whis - per what you'll bring to me; tell me if you can.

Children, Go Where I Send Thee

Spiritual

Teacher Duet: (Student plays 1 octave higher)

Joseph, Dearest Joseph

Traditional German Carol

Teacher Duet: (Student plays 2 octaves higher than written)

*Note to Teacher: Teacher pedals when playing duet.

Angels We Have Heard on High

Traditional French Carol

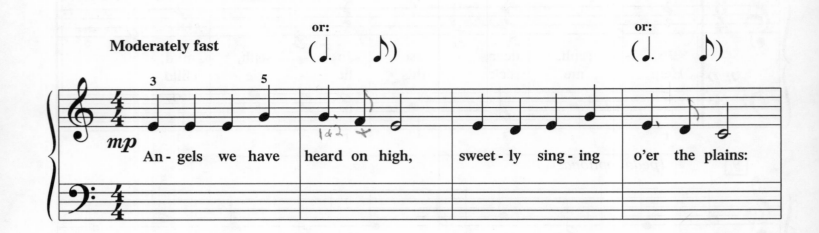

An - gels we have heard on high, sweet - ly sing - ing o'er the plains:

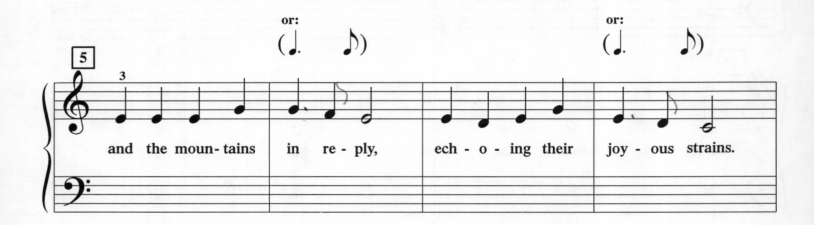

and the moun - tains in re - ply, ech - o - ing their joy - ous strains.

Teacher Duet: (Student plays 1 octave higher)

This arrangement Copyright © 1995 The FJH Music Company Inc.
International Copyright Secured.   Made in U.S.A.   All Rights Reserved.

Pa-ta-pan

French Carol

Moderately fast (in 2)

L.H. 1 octave lower throughout

Wil - lie, bring your lit - tle drum, al - so Rob - in,

bring your flute. Beat the drum and blow "toot,

Teacher Duet: (Student plays as written)

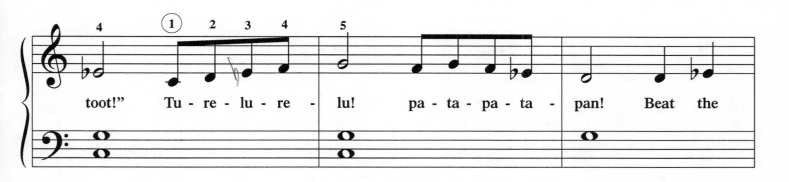

toot!" Tu - re - lu - re - lu!   pa - ta - pa - ta - pan!   Beat the

drum and blow the   flute, join___ in, let___   none be

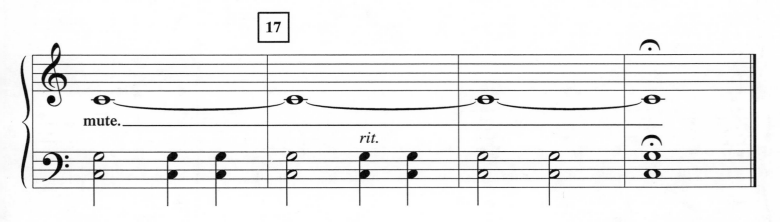

mute.___

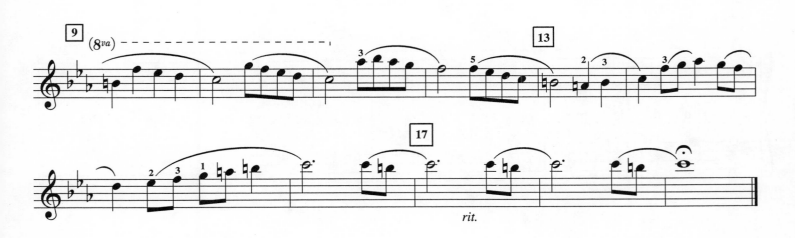

Jingle Bells

James Pierpont

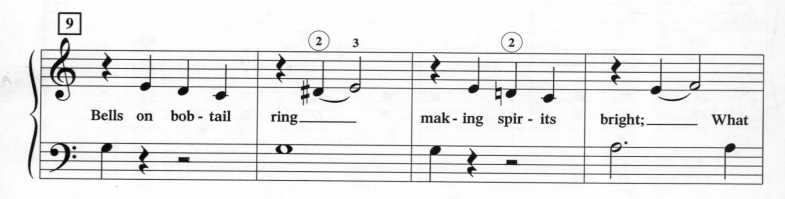